Teed Off!

A Modern Guide to Golf

D0104860

Tom Carey

SOURCEBOOKS HYSTERIA™
AN IMPRINT OF SOURCEBOOKS, INC.™
NAPERVILLE, ILLINOIS

Published by Sourcebooks Hysteria, an imprint of Sourcebooks, Inc.
P.O. Box 4410, Naperville, Illinois 60567-4410
(630) 961-3900
FAX: (630) 961-2168
www.sourcebooks.com

Library of Congress Cataloging-in-Publication Data
Carey, Tom.
  Teed off! : the modern guide to golf / Tom Carey.
     p. cm.
  ISBN-13: 978-1-4022-0520-0
  ISBN-10: 1-4022-0520-1
  1. Golf—Humor. 2. Golf—Caricature and cartoons. I. Title.

PN6231.G68C38 2006
818'.5402—dc22

                                              2005025023

          Printed and bound in the United States of America
               VP 10 9 8 7 6 5 4 3 2 1

For my dad, who taught me everything
I know about golf and a good deal of
what I know about life, too.
Thanks, Chop.

Table of Contents

Introduction:

Golf: Harmless Game or Evil Curse? 1

Chapter 1:

A History of the Game: How Did It
Begin...And Is It Too Late to Stop It? 5

Chapter 2:

Equipment: Are Fuzzy Alligator
Head Covers Really Necessary? 15

Chapter 3:

Playing the Game: People
Pay Money to Do This? 37

Chapter 4:

Where to Play: A Course
Is a Course, of Course, of Course 55

Chapter 5:

How Do You Get to

Pebble Beach? Practice 67

Chapter 6:

Professional Golf:

People *Get Paid* to Do This? 75

Chapter 7:

Golfspeak: A Glossary of Terms,

Definitions, and Swear Words 99

Chapter 8:

The Ten Commandments

of Modern Golf 111

About the Author 122

Golf:
Harmless Game or Evil Curse?

The game of golf is a mysterious thing. Its history is shrouded in legend, myth, and lore. It is a game rich in arcane rules and time-honored customs; the traditional pastime of gentlemen and ladies of breeding for more than a hundred years. It is a test of skill, a test of nerve, and a test of imagination.

It is a test of skill when you've got 165 yards left from a flyer lie to a tiny little green, with a pin tucked behind one of those ridiculous Robert Trent Jones, you-gotta-be-freakin'-kidding-me railroad-tie bunkers. It is a test of nerve when you need to drain a sidehill five-footer on some car-hood-fast, 13-on-the-Stimpmeter green to save triple bogey. And it is a test of imagination when you've got to explain to the wife why the new set of perimeter-weighted irons you got was more important than last month's car payment.

Yes, golf has evolved tremendously in the last hundred years. Equipment has changed, rules have changed, and hardly anyone wears a kilt anymore.

This book was written to help today's golfer become a golfer unbound by ancient rules and old traditions. A golfer unafraid to wipe the beer from his face, tee it up with his naked-lady tee, swing from the heels with his brand-new, $600 TaylorMade driver with a head as big as a Volkswagen, and watch proudly as his mighty clout sails into the great beyond. A golfer unafraid, then, to take a mulligan.

**Young Tom Morris
Invents Golf**

A History of the Game:
How Did It Begin...And Is It Too Late to Stop It?

The Morrises: Young Tom, Olde Tom, and Other People with Ridiculous Names

The game of golf was invented in St. Andrews, a small seaside village in Scotland, in the late nineteenth century by Olde Tom Morris and his son, Young Tom Morris. (The Scots are notoriously unimaginative when it comes to naming their kids.) They were sitting by Loch Ness one typically dark, rainy afternoon with their cameras waiting for the monster to surface, when Young Tom, bored with trying to keep the rain off his camera lens, absentmindedly took a swipe at a stone on the beach with his walking stick.

Young Tom Morris Discovers The "Yips"

As fate would have it, he struck the stone a solid blow, and it flew straight at an old, gnarled oak tree some yards away. The two Morrises were intrigued. As they walked up to the tree Olde Tom said, "I'll bet ye five bob ye kin nawt strike the tree wi' another stroke."

An intense look came over Young Tom's ruddy features. Though the rock lay just three feet from the tree, Young Tom began to shake and sweat from the pressure of his father's challenge.

"C'mon lad! Et's but a wee bit away! What the matter? Can't ye take the pressure, ya sniveling pantywaist?!" Young Tom brandished his walking stick menacingly and growled at his father, "Shut yer gob, mon, or I'll shut it for ya!" His blood racing, his heart pounding, Young Tom waggled his walking stick at least a dozen times before he was able to swing at the stone again. And of course, he missed the little putt. Furious, he smashed his stick against the tree, breaking it to pieces, and screamed, "It's the devil's oon game we've invented, and I'll ne'er play it agin!"

Of course, he bought a new stick and was whacking stones on the beach again the very next day. Which is how Young Tom Morris invented the "yips" and Olde Tom Morris invented the Nassau.

Golf in America: The Plague Spreads

For years the Morrises had the game of golf to themselves. They laid out eighteen holes along the beach at St. Andrews, and they were content smacking stones with their walking sticks and screaming hideous insults at one another.

Then one surprisingly sunny afternoon, as they trudged along the beach looking for a lost ball, they stumbled upon a family of vacationing Americans. Otto Bunker, a tailor, and his seamstress wife, Anita, were sunbathing in the middle of the sixth hole. It was a gruesome sight as the Bunkers were a decidedly chubby pair and they exhibited vast glowing expanses of alabaster skin that had obviously seen no sunshine for years. The Scotsmen were livid.

Shading their eyes from the powerful glare, they approached the Americans. "You kin naye lay aboot here, ya stupid gits!" cried Young Tom. "This is a gahf links!"

Otto, who prided himself on having a cheerful demeanor, just nodded enthusiastically and smiled, though he had no idea what it was that the snarling, red-faced Scotsman was screaming about. Still, he felt he should make some kind of reply. Grinning, in what he considered a very friendly way, he looked at the enraged Morrises in their plaid kilts and asked them to pose for a photo.

"The folks back home will love a shot of you fellas in those skirts," he said, draping his flabby, sunburned arms across the shoulders of the seething Scotsmen.

Sadly for the grinning American tailor, Young Tom Morris could hold his temper no longer. Just as Mrs. Bunker yelled "Say *haggis*!" and clicked her camera, Young Tom clouted the tailor with his club, forever after called a "cleek" for the sound that it made on Otto's skull. The Bunkers' attorney later used the photograph to win them a large cash settlement and the U.S. rights to the game of golf.

Poor Young Tom Morris was plagued forever after by nightmares in which chubby, pale Americans in bathing suits lay down in his line every time he tried to line up a putt.

The Bunkers: The First Family of U.S. Golf

So it came to be that Otto and Anita Bunker came home to New Jersey the proud owners of two sets of golf clubs, several dozen nice, round stones, and the right to build golf courses in the USA.

The Bunkers had plenty of time for their new hobby because, although they were both expert clothiers, each was unutterably color-blind. Unscrupulous wholesalers had for years forced all their ugliest material on the unsuspecting Bunkers, who were unable to sell a stitch of the awful clothing they made.

One typically slow day at the store, Otto was fooling around with his new golf clubs when he had a sudden burst of inspiration. In an effort to drum up business, Otto placed a newspaper ad offering a free round of golf to anyone who bought a pair of their very ugly

**Otto Bunker,
Founder of American Golf**

trousers. A couple of adventurous folks saw the ad and gave the new game, and the pants, a try. In no time they were hooked on golf.

Word got around about the addictive game, and soon the Bunkers' store and golf course became very, very busy indeed. Before long, every tailor for miles had built a golf course and the countryside was crawling with scores of golfers, bashing their new golf balls, swinging their new golf clubs, and buying pair after pair of the ugliest, loudest, tackiest, most horrible pants ever seen in North America.

Golf, as we know it today, was born.

The "Featherie"

Equipment:
Are Fuzzy Alligator Head Covers Really Necessary?

The Balls: Have You Got 'Em?

The first real golf balls were developed by the Morrises because they quickly got fed up with breaking their expensive walking sticks on rocks. The beaches of Scotland seemed about to disappear forever under piles of broken walking sticks, scattered there by the Morris boys and their golfing buddies. Then

something marvelous occurred: the invention of the first golf ball, the "featherie."

It happened that Young Tom Morris was the family cook. One day, in the course of preparing a goose for dinner, he noticed that goose feathers shrank considerably when boiled. He stuffed some inside a cover of stitched leather, and when they dried, the feathers expanded to form a tight, solid, perfect little ball.

Production of the featherie was very slow until Tom's mom, Olde Lady Morris (what else?), suggested that he remove the goose feathers from the goose *before* boiling. This change sped up production of the new ball immensely and saved many golf ball makers from having their eyes pecked out by enraged boiling geese.

The Featherie Era lasted until about 1900 when bird lovers, concerned about the fast-dwindling

Scottish goose population, discovered a material called "gutta percha" (I am not making these names up by the way) in the Far East.

The gutta percha golf ball (known as the "guttie") was cheap, and it flew farther and lasted longer than the featherie. Sporting goods companies quickly realized that a serious golf enthusiast would sell his children for five more yards on his tee ball—an industry tenet that still applies today—and they began to import tons of the new balls. Soon golfers everywhere had switched to the guttie.

The ensuing decades saw the rise and fall of balls made of rubber (the "mooshie"), plastic (the "gooshie"), and with centers made of cork (the "corkie"), steel (the "steelie"), glycerine (the "mooshie-gooshie"), and even water (the "Jim-Bob").

By the 1960s, manufacturers had settled on two styles of balls, one made of a space-age material called "balata" and one made of a space-age material called "surlyn," thus beginning the Space-Age Material Era of golf ball making and ending the Stupid Nickname Era.

The difference between the two balls was vast. The Balata was preferred by the better player. It was softer and a good player could control the spin he put on the ball. A talented golf pro could make a Balata ball fade, draw, jump, hop, and sing two verses of "Raindrops Keep Fallin' on My Head."

Unfortunately, Balata balls were also easy to damage. The slightest mishit would cause a Balata ball to slice wide open and plummet to the earth, spilling its innards, gasping its dying breath. The ball could be replaced, of course, but the player bore the expense. Even a good player might plow through a dozen Balata balls each round. Still, good players (and those who wanted others to think they were good players) played Balata.

The surlyn ball, on the other hand, was virtually uncutable. It also flew farther. These balls were so hard and unyielding that the Morris boys would have been right at home banging on them instead of their original rocks.

"In a perfect world," golfers everywhere dreamt, "we wouldn't have to choose. We'd have a golf ball with the durability and length of Surlyn and the soft feel and controllability of Balata."

Good old American ingenuity finally came through in the mid-1990s. The golf ball was perfected, allowing even the worst hacker with the most cringe-inducing flog to blast his driver up with the pros. Armed with the new balls, of course, pros were now able to smash their drivers such huge distances that thousands of golf courses became obsolete overnight.

The goose population, meanwhile, increased a thousandfold due to the extinction of their chief predator, Scottish golf ball makers. The trauma inflicted upon their ancestors has not been forgotten by subsequent generations of geese, who now flock to golf courses everywhere to "fertilize" the fairways, clog the water hazards, and generally make life miserable for golfers.

Some relief may be in sight, however. Several U.S. senators, who had some very expensive shoes ruined by goose poop at a celebrity Pro-Am Tournament in which they were playing, recently proposed the "Kill All the Damn Geese" bill. If it passes, this law will make it legal once again to boil geese alive.

The Clubs: $1,000 Worth of Graphite Garden Tools

Early clubs had names like the Moody, the Geek, the Panghorne, and the Slap-Doodle. (If you think it's hard to hit a 1-iron, you should try hitting a Slap-Doodle.) The shafts of these clubs were wooden and, though they were difficult for the average player to hit, they did make a satisfying snap when broken over the knee or heaved against a tree.

Unfortunately, they also often broke during the swing, which could be very disconcerting for the other players in the group. Many golfers of this era were tragically killed by flying remnants of shattered wooden shafts, a public relations problem that threatened the popularity of the new game. It was very, very dangerous to play golf at this time.

It also turned out to be a serious problem for rule-makers. The newly formed United States Golf Association solved this dilemma in one of its first and most controversial decisions. The USGA ruled that players could take a free drop two club lengths away from dead or injured players. They also allowed the manufacture of steel shafts.

Today's golf clubs are made from materials like graphite, magnesium, and cadmium borate ascorbic acid. They allow the average player to hit it deep into the rough and to reach previously unreachable hazards. And some can pick up police-band radio.

By the Numbers
The Driver

The driver is a club used to tee off. It is the longest and most expensive club in most players' bags. The shaft length and clubhead size of drivers has gotten so out of hand that luxury auto manufacturers have begun altering the interior dimensions of their new vehicles to accommodate driver's drivers. Ironically, for most players, the driver produces a high, short, soft shot, especially on holes with a water hazard in front of the tee.

The Fairway Woods

The fairway woods are the more lofted clubs that a player uses when he has hit his tee shot but is still a long way from the green. For most players, that will be several times a hole. Many players find that these fairway woods (now virtually all made of metal, another of golf's little ironies) are easier to hit than long irons and so carry nothing but woods in their bags. This has led to the invention of such ridiculous clubs as the wedge wood and the 27-wood.

AS A MATTER OF FACT, I DO HAVE A PUTTING WOOD. WHY?

The Irons

Irons are traditionally numbered 1 through 9 (since the end of the Stupid Nickname Era, anyway). Each one is a bit longer and less lofted than the club numerically following and each is designed to go about ten yards farther. It is vitally important to know exactly how far you hit each club so you know how enraged to get when you leave an approach shot short, buried in a bunker.

The 1-Iron

This club is very difficult to hit due to its low loft and long shaft. There is a famous golf joke that has Lee Trevino walking off a golf course in the rain, holding a 1-iron over his head to protect him from lightning. "Even God can't hit a 1-iron," says Trevino, according to this gag. You will hear this joke every time you enter a golf course locker room. Which is one good reason to change your shoes in the parking lot.

The Pitching Wedge

The pitching wedge is a very lofted club used primarily around the green. It is used to launch a low, knuckling, line-drive type of shot.

Hitting The "Wedge"

The Sand Wedge

The sand wedge will produce the same kind of shot as the pitching wedge, even out of a bunker!

The Putter

The putter is used to roll the ball along the ground. It is a very important club because most players will use it three or four times on each hole. This is the favorite club of many golfers, and some have been known to keep dozens—or hundreds—stashed away in their basements.

Get a Grip! The Golf Glove

The golf glove is a very important piece of equipment that no golfer should be without. Hand sewn from the skin of goat embryos (I'm not making that up, either—I could never invent something that gross), the golf glove keeps the modern golfer's delicate hand from getting blisters and provides for a powerful grip. It also keeps his left hand pale and white while his right hand gets a dark tan, which lets everyone he meets know that he is a proud and well-appointed golfer. Or a Michael Jackson impersonator.

You should only remove a golf glove for putting or drinking beer. The latter is especially important because when it's really hot and your beer can gets all sweaty it could cause your golf glove to get wet and slippery. This, in turn, can cause the club to fly out of your hand during a swing and possibly injure the girl who drives the beer cart, thus depriving you of beer for the rest of the round. So remember to always remove your golf glove when drinking beer.

The Pull Cart

This is the traditional method of golf club transport. It has the convenience of an electric cart (i.e., wheels) yet still allows you to say that you are "getting some exercise." As though a five-mile walk in six hours could be considered exercise. As a calorie burner, golf ranks right up there with gin rummy.

The nice thing about a pull cart is that there is plenty of room on it for all the gizmos you will be receiving for birthdays and Christmas for the rest of your life once people find out you're a serious golfer. Grateful that they no longer need to spend time searching for the perfect gift, family members will deluge you with plastic beer can holders, naked-lady tees, exploding balls, and fuzzy-faced animal-head club covers.

Colorful Umbrella
(for poking thrown clubs out of trees)

Funny Animal head covers (xmas gift 1998)

TV to keep up with pro tournament

Tee, ball, card, cigarette holder (xmas gift 1997)

Fuzzy Dice

Horn to "motivate" slow players

Ball retriever (xmas 2000)

Walkman with Cybernetics tape (xmas 2001)

Exotic bag tags

Beer Holder (xmas gift 2003)

Cooler on wheels (with extra beer)

Knobby treads
(for "accidentally" rolling over opponent's line)

You'll feel obligated to use these items, especially when your six-year-old daughter looks up at you with her big brown eyes and trembling lower lip and asks why Daddy doesn't have on the "I ♥ Golf" hat she got him for his birthday. So you'll wear the hat, which labels you as a hopeless dork on the golf course, as surely as does the use of iron covers, golf ball retrievers, and cargo shorts with a special pocket for your golf tees.

The Bag: If You Can Carry It Yourself, It's Too Small

Just as a woman needs a handbag to fit every occasion, a golfer needs a golf bag to do the same. (Feel free to use this analogy when you have to explain to the wife how you really needed that new eel-skin job with the fur-lined pockets.)

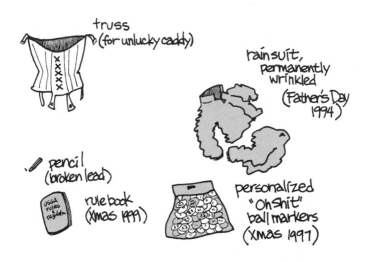

truss
(for unlucky caddy)

rain suit,
permanently
wrinkled
(Father's Day
1994)

pencil
(broken lead)

USGA rules regulation

rule book
(Xmas 1999)

personalized
"Oh Shit"
ball markers
(Xmas 1997)

scorecard from
the time you almost
broke 100

tape measure
(for closest to the
pin arguments)

two orange balls
(for water holes)

bag of personalized
naked lady tees
(Xmas gift 1989)

Inside The Golf Bag

The Sunday Bag

The Sunday bag is a small, lightweight bag about the size of your son's SpongeBob SquarePants backpack. It is designed to hold a couple of clubs and a few balls and to fold up neatly to fit in your car's glove box. This is important for those times when you're between sales calls and want to sneak in a

few holes before lunch. You can then sling the Sunday bag over your shoulder and climb the fence of the nearby muni and play a few without paying. And should the ranger chase after you in his electric cart, you can run very quickly with this lightweight bag on your back.

The Country Club Bag

You'll know you've really made it in the world of golf when you proudly purchase a golf bag that costs more than you paid for your first house (and is twice as roomy). The country club bag is more than a receptacle for your clubs, balls, sweaters, Band-Aids, socks, instruction manuals, gloves, visors, rain suit, umbrella, shaving kit, rule book, and tape measure. Much more. It is a statement. It says, "I have money." It says, "I love golf." But mostly it says, "I can afford to pay someone else to carry my clubs."

Letting Out The Shaft

Playing the Game:
People *Pay Money* to Do This?

Driving: Getting Really Teed Off

In the beginning there is the drive. There is nothing more satisfying than the sound and feel of a well-struck tee shot. Most of you, I know, will simply have to take my word for that.

The tee is a plot of ground where a player may place his ball on a little wooden peg called, surprisingly enough, a tee. Using a tee allows the player to sweep his club complete-ly under the ball, like a magician pulling a tablecloth out from under a pitcher of water.

The idea, on the tee, is for the player to take the biggest, longest, most unwieldy club in his bag (the driver) and have a really wild swipe at the ball. Even if his tee shot flies deep into the woods or far out of bounds, he will have released from inside all the rage and aggres-sion that has built up since he missed that short par putt on the previous hole.

Once this pressure has been released, he can chase down his errant shot in relatively good spirits. Players who spend a lot of time on the tee futzing around with trivialities—like aiming, for instance—end up safely in the fair-way a lot, which defeats the spirit and pur-pose of the game.

Fairway Shots: A Very Short Section

Occasionally, even a player who swings so hard on the tee that he actually screws himself into the ground will hit his tee ball into the fairway. It happens so infrequently, however, that to go into a detailed explanation of fairway play here would be rather pointless.

Hazards of Golf: Over the River and Through the Woods

There is a saying in golf that "trees are 90 percent air." You'll always hear this after you've blasted your tee ball so deep into the forest lining of your golf course that you half expect to stumble across a Tin Man begging in a squeaky voice for his oil can. As you struggle to decide whether to chip safely and sanely back into the fairway or whether it might be smarter to try for a low-rising, 195-yard running hook over a bush, under a branch, and around a water hazard, you will hear this "90 percent air" stuff from your opponents. They say this because they are sportsmen and lovers of the game, and because it's a thrill to see someone pull off a glorious one-in-a-million trick shot to save par from a densely wooded jail. Also, they want your money.

Then next time an opponent sidles over to you and smugly opines that trees are 90 percent air, tell him that humans are 90 percent water and you're going to drive your car through him to get a wash.

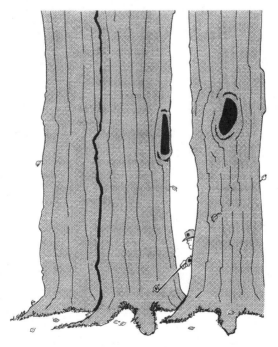

"Trees Are 90% Air"

Water Hazards and Sand Traps

The water hazard has been a traditional grave-yard for errant golf balls since the days when the Morrises and their pals were banging featheries into the Atlantic Ocean. St. Andrews is a "links" golf course—nine holes straight out and nine holes straight back home—which means water on the left side of every hole on the front nine. This was a serious problem for Young Tom Morris, since he tended to hook the ball, while all the other players at the club hit controlled fades. For years, Young Tom pounded balls into the briny deep on the front nine while his partners chuckled and took his money.

One night, after a particularly difficult round, the angry young man took a shovel to the right side of the back nine of the course, determined to dig and dig until he struck water,

The Water Hazard
Scotland, Circa 1871

thus equalizing the situation. Unfortunately, no matter where he dug or how deep he went, all he dug up was sand.

Come morning, the first foursome on the links found Young Tom sprawled in one of the dozens of sand pits he had dug. He was fast asleep and having his recurring nightmare about the Bunker family, screaming out loud, "The Bunkers, the Bunkers! They're everywhere!"

Being Scotsmen, and too cheap to repair the damage to their golf course, the rules committee convened and decided that the sand pits would stay. From that day forward, it became traditional for golf courses to be built with "Bunkers everywhere!"

The Short Game: Chilly Dips and Fried Eggs

The Short Game is a term describing those crucial little shots around the green. For most golfers, it is also a description of their tee shots, but let us not dwell on this.

The Chip Shot

When a player is ten yards or closer to the green, he must hit a chip shot. What makes a chip shot different from other ten-yard shots is that a chip shot is *actually only meant to go that far.*

The Pitch Shot

The pitch shot is a high, soft shot, which will stop quickly as it lands gently in a bunker in someone's footprint. Which leaves you with…

The Sand Shot

What to do when your ball is buried so deep in the sand that you need a permit from the gas company to play it? Any pro will tell you that sand shots are "easy." Use the sand wedge, a heavy, lofted club, to inflict the maximum amount of pain on any pro who says this too often.

Putting: Yippy-Ay-Yay

Ever since that fateful day in St. Andrews when Young Tom Morris yipped his first putt by the oak tree, golfers everywhere have sweated, twitched, and gagged over the simple task of rolling a ball into a hole. Golfers will try anything to improve their putting. When Sam Snead began squatting over his putts croquet-style in a vain attempt to cure his yips, millions of weekend hackers began squatting over their putts, too. The USGA quickly outlawed this practice for being "exceedingly stupid."

When Jack Nicklaus won the Masters in 1986 (at the advanced age of 46) with a putter blade that was substantially larger than his own head, millions of golfers began toting twenty-five pound "Nicklaus-Head" blades. These, too, were outlawed by the USGA but not before a startling number of players and caddies were felled by hernias.

The current trend among the putting-impaired is the extra-long putter. Seniors whose arms have become too short to read their Viagra prescriptions can now see their shoelaces in startling detail and easily make their three-footers using this club. It makes the

player look tremendously silly when hitting a putt, but then, most of them are already accustomed to looking tremendously silly on a golf course.

The "Over 40" Putter

Blowin' in the Wind: Braving the Elements

Sooner or later you're going to get stuck playing in the rain (especially if you have a regular tee time reserved with a major credit card). When faced with a fast-moving incoming storm, my Dad used to say, "Hell, son, you *know* it never rains on a golf course! Let's keep playing!" That was before he got hit by lightning while lining up a ten-footer for birdie. If you think South Florida was a disaster area after Hurricane Andrew, you should see my old man's putting stroke these days.

Any player who's really serious about golf will learn to play wearing boots, ski gloves, hand warmers, polypropylene long johns, three sweaters, two jackets, a scarf, and earmuffs. This can actually be a blessing. When you find yourself too bound up to take a swing that remotely resembles something golf-like and your tee ball veers wildly and strikes the only other person loony enough to be on a golf course that day, you'll be too wrapped up in extra clothing to be recognizable, thus avoiding potentially costly litigation.

Foul Weather Golf

Keeping Score: The Foot Wedge and Pencil Iron

Keeping score in golf can be a complicated proposition. Like many things in life, a golf score is open to interpretation. Oh, there are purists who insist that all putts be holed and all shots counted, but as Al Capone used to say when delivering unordered cases of liquor to terrified speakeasy owners during Prohibition, "Everything's negotiable, right?"

For instance, let's say you play a hole thusly: You flog your tee ball into a waste area and then take several brutish swipes at it before it finally pops out, jarring loose a bush, three rocks, and a hornet's nest in the process. Then, you skull a 5-iron into a greenside bunker. From there it's two or three more swipes just to get the damn thing out. Disgusted, you carelessly slap your lag putt past the hole, miss the comebacker, and then finish things off by playing green hockey around the hole, scraping the ball back and forth until it finally drops. You *may* want to *estimate* your final total.

"I *think* I had a 7," you'll say (when asked), providing not so much a score as a neighborhood. A ballpark figure, if you will. By feigning memory loss, you have effectively thrown yourself upon the mercy of your peers, who know that they too may have an attack of "golfer's amnesia" before the round is over. They will likely give you the imaginary score you claim without making a peep. And, hey, let's face it, you deserve no more than a 7! I mean, if it wasn't for the damn rough (that should have been cut days ago) and that bad lie in the sand (does anybody around here ever use a rake!?), you probably would have gotten a 5! Certainly no more than a 6! I mean you *never* get more than a 6 on this hole. So, when you think about it, taking a 7 is actually an act of great humility and decency.

Also, when reporting your final score in the bar after your round, it is important to add a short addendum. You didn't have a "94." You had a "94-with-2-out-of-bounds-on-13-and-4-3-putts-on-the-front." This lets all the golfers within earshot know that it was cruel fate that caused your drive on the twelfth to fly into that condo owner's bowl of Rice Krispies, not your own wicked slice.

Where to Play:
A Course Is a Course, of Course, of Course

The Public Course

The public course is the place where most folks get their first taste of the wondrous game of golf. Most of these bare, brown, over-played dirt tracks are run by benevolent fellows who are in business because they love the game and want to bring it to the greatest number of people. Also because local zoning laws won't let them plow the place under and put up luxury condos.

The greens fees at these courses are low, which makes them frighteningly popular. This is why the most coveted prize in golf isn't the Ryder Cup or the Claret Jug. It's the Permanent Tee Time. Win one and you'll play every Saturday at 5 a.m. (or 4:08 p.m. or midnight or whatever time they damn well tell you to) from March to December. It doesn't matter if a tornado or snowstorm hits or you suffer cardiac arrest. If you don't find a sub before they load you into the ambulance, the public course manager will auction your place off to the highest bidder. And they'll have it sold before your doctor can say, "quadruple bypass."

See, there are a million golf junkies just like you, jonesing so bad that they'll get up every Saturday morning at 4:15 and pay actual U.S.

currency to shoot 147 in a six-hour death march around a course where the fairways are harder than an interstate expressway, the greens are bumpier than a teenager's face, and the "sand" traps are filled with a substance that can only be described as dirt.

The Country Club

There are some very distinct differences between playing golf at a crowded, low-quality public course and playing at an exclusive, well-manicured country club. About 50,000 very distinct differences, actually.

A country club is an organization of doctors, lawyers, and men who have not yet squandered their wives' large inheritances, who have gotten tired of waiting in the damp, frozen dawn for a tee time at some over-played, worn-out public dog track. These men write

Harvard-tuition-sized checks each year for the privilege of waiting in the damp frozen dawn for a tee time at their own private club. Plus, they get free coffee and sweet rolls.

But to a serious golfer, the lure of the country club is much stronger than the continental breakfast. In addition to having a well-groomed course to play, there's the complimentary Pinaud body talc in the shower, the freedom to tell incredibly offensive sexist jokes in the card room (especially important for judges and politicians), and a swell plastic bag tag with their club affiliation on it (so airline baggage handlers will look at his golf bag and say "Hey, this guy's rich! Let's rifle the pockets!").

Resort Golf

The resort golf course caters to those golfers who are on a golf vacation. This course is predominantly found in the south and south-west, where year-round warm weather tempts the snowbound northern golfer to throw caution—and his kid's college fund—to the wind to play golf in February. Resort courses usually feature "package deals," which the desperate snowbird and three of his buddies can book online with the click of a mouse. Renting a "golf course view" two-bedroom condo, the intrepid foursome follows an itinerary designed to cram as much golf into four days as they might experience in three years of regular play.

A sample itinerary follows:

Golf Trip Itinerary

4:15 a.m.—Limo Arrives

Ride to airport sitting atop golf bags because someone forgot to order a stretch limo with extra trunk space. Suspicious and pungent odors emanate from one partner, who had Mexican food the night before.

5:00 a.m.—Airport Check-In

Agree to over-tip skycap at airport to make sure that all golf clubs arrive at destination promptly. Stand in security line manned, incredibly, by a single security person. Try to restrain amazement, anger, and snide remarks about shoe bombs as three out of four of you are singled out for "extra security measures." Thankfully, fourth member is the Mexican food guy, who rushes to the nearby men's room.

6:00 a.m.—Arrive at Gate

Flight will be delayed, of course, making first tee time highly doubtful. Consternation abounds when group realizes that even though they all agreed to over-tip the skycap, nobody was designated to actually do it. Realize that golf bags may be headed to Taiwan.

7:40 a.m.—Flight Departs

Relax and begin talking excitedly about golf as the little turbo prop lifts shakily off and the airport Starbucks *Venti Americanos* kick in. Notice that the entire plane is filled with overfed, overcaffeinated, middle-aged men in Ashworth sweaters and Titleist caps, talking excitedly about golf. Notice flight attendant swallowing three Advil.

10:50 a.m.—Flight Arrives

Two members of the group stand in line at the car rental counter to rent a minivan along with twenty other golfers who have also rented minivans and who are all playing the same place you are. The other two wait with trepidation in baggage claim for the clubs. One bag arrives in good shape. One bag is split open, but the clubs are undamaged. One bag is badly mangled with stray pieces of clubs hanging out. One does not arrive.

11:15 a.m.—Drive to Course

It's a one-hour drive to the resort where you are staying, but you're determined to be on the tee in forty-five minutes. One player drives 25 miles per hour over the limit after the others agree to pay any speeding tickets. Two players change clothes in the van and put on golf shoes while the fourth pouts because his clubs did not arrive.

12:00 p.m.

Park the van and race across the parking lot with your clubs, only to find that the course starter is running about an hour and a half behind schedule. Realize with relief that you have time for a relaxing lunch and some time at the driving range, especially important since it's March and no one in your group has swung a club since October.

12:30 p.m.—Lunch

Sandwiches arrive and one guy orders a round of beers. No one wants to be accused of not pitching in his fair share, so each man takes a turn buying a round of drinks.

1:30 p.m.—Tee Off

Stumble to first tee with two minutes to spare after four beers in forty-five minutes. There's no time for a warm-up, so each man jams a tee in the turf and swings away. Two balls go out of bounds right, one is popped up to the ladies tee, and one guy picks up after his practice swing with a dislocated shoulder.

4:00 p.m.—Halfway House

The group is finally getting into the groove after two dozen lost balls and a couple of stern warnings from the marshals to "pick up the pace." Group celebrates with another round of beers and six extras in a plastic bag of ice "for the road."

7:30 p.m.—18th Hole

Finally stumble to the finish, playing the last two holes in the dark. Beer cart girl has actually stopped going to other groups and is happily riding along, counting her tip money, and agreeing, for an extra $50, to help players find their condo in the dark and to drive the minivan there as well.

8:30 p.m.—Arrive at Condo

Tip cart girl again. Unload minivan. Order pizza. Shower. More beers. ESPN.

10:00 p.m.—Cards

Argue about whether to play poker, gin, or spades.

10:15 p.m.—Lights Out

Give up on cards and collapse into bed.

11:30 p.m.—Change Rooms

Two snorers are put together so the two non-snorers can sleep.

6:00 a.m.—Wake Up

Tee time is 6:30 a.m. You'll get coffee and a bagel at the course.

Repeat daily until departure.

How Do You Get to Pebble Beach? Practice.

The Swing: Flying Elbows and Rusty Gates

No physical movement in the history of sports has been as over-analyzed, as over-dissected, over-diagrammed, and as relentlessly studied as the golf swing. Golf magazines devote hundreds of pages to controversial issues like head tilt and thumb placement. High-speed photography, once used only in military research, has emerged as a whole new field in golf. The U.S. army now lures young people into the service with the promise that after they're discharged they will be highly trained photographers ready to start a lucrative career shooting ten-frames-per-second photos of pro golfers for instructional articles.

In reality, the golf swing is not that complex. It's a simple matter of keeping your head down, keeping your eye on the ball, keeping your left arm straight, keeping your left foot perpendicular to the intended line of flight, keeping your right elbow tucked in, keeping the swing path inside out, keeping the club horizontal at the top of the backswing, shifting your weight, delaying your release, hitting down and through the ball, staying balanced, and following through to the target.

De-Ranged: On the Ol' Rock Pile

The driving range is an empty lot where golfers pay real, hard-earned, after-tax cash for the privilege of pounding rock-hard chunks of red-striped ovoids into an empty field. There are sixteenth-century Hieronymus Bosch murals depicting the tortures of hell that resemble nothing so much as the huddled masses gouging up the Astroturf mats at the local Stop-N-Sock.

The driving range proprietor will gleefully sell you a wire basket full of nicked and dented objects suspiciously similar in appearance to Scottish beach rocks for about $10. If the nation's interstates were paved with the material from which these balls are made, highways would be so resilient that construction workers from coast to coast would be thrown out of work and forced to find somewhere else to sit in their trucks and eat doughnuts.

Periodically, a minimum-wage kid in a hockey helmet will drive out onto the range in a souped-up tractor covered with chicken wire to scoop up the "balls" so that they may be hit again. And again. And again.

The range won't improve your game much, but dinging a few off the pick-up cart may help you develop a punch shot that you can use when you end up under one of those "90 percent air" trees.

The Off-Season: Rug Putting and Garage Golf

The truly dedicated golfer maintains a fierce and demanding practice schedule in the off-season; the off-season being those few weeks when the average temperature is below ten degrees Fahrenheit. (If it's warmer than that, you play, dammit!)

Rather than risk losing your swing over a few months' rest, as a dedicated player you must set up your own in-home practice area. If you are lucky enough to live in a home or apartment with high ceilings and shag carpeting, you just need to hang netting over all the walls and you'll be ready to hit golf balls whenever and wherever the mood strikes.

If you don't have high ceilings (or if you're married), you'll have to use the garage for your practice area. Just pick up one of those huge nets you'll find advertised in the back of golf magazines next to the ads for illegal balls that go 500 yards and the "Hypnotize Your Way to a Better Swing" videotapes. They only cost a few thousand bucks and are easy to assemble, as long as you're a German auto mechanic and have access to a variety of exotic power tools.

Spend an hour a day in the off-season hitting balls into your net, and by spring you'll have locked into muscle-memory at least twenty new and difficult-to-change swing habits. Your reflexes will get a workout, too, as you dodge the errant golf balls ricocheting around your garage.

Come spring, you can dismantle the thing and toss it into that rusting metal shed you put up in the backyard where it can gather dust next to the weight bench, rowing machine, and stationary bike that you also bought and now never use.

Keeping your short game in shape in the off-season is a much easier proposition. Simply shave down a chunk of carpeting in your home, say, the living room area, to the speed of a well-kept putting green. Then you can practice your putting all the time. If you pull up the carpeting and stuff objects under it (a dish, a glass, stacks of old magazines, the cat) you can create real bends and breaks, thereby customizing your little indoor putting surface and making it just like a real green.

Again, this is only for those of you who are not married. Or have no wish to ever be married. Or who wish to soon not be married.

Professional Golf:
People *Get Paid* to Do This?

The Touring Pro: Money for Nuthin', Sticks for Free

The first professional golfers were usually former caddies who spent their formative years toting the bags of rich men with too many pairs of bad pants and too much time on their hands. These soon-to-be-pros were clever enough to notice a few things about the rich

The Teaching Pro

folks. One, they loved golf. Two, they bet big cash. Three, most of them couldn't make a par if you put them on the ladies tee and gave them two mulligans.

The enterprising young caddy would quickly learn this game that rich folks found so difficult. If he were enterprising enough, he would play matches against the rich folks and regularly separate them from large wads of cash. Often, after many humiliations, all the rich folks in the area would get together and agree to make a lump-sum monthly payment to the young man if he would just hang around and *not* play golf with them. In this way, professional golf began.

Most pros settled into country club life, teaching golf lessons, overcharging members for shirts, hats, and golf umbrellas, drinking at the clubhouse bar, and carrying on illicit affairs with the bored wives of club members, who spent every waking hour on the golf course.

Sooner or later, even the doofiest of rich guys would figure out what was going on and realize that something would have to be done about the club pro "problem."

As the rich businessmen traveled, meeting and talking with other rich businessmen, it became clear to them that this club-pro, bored-wife, expensive-golf-shirt phenomenon was occurring all over the United States. The rich guys decided it was time to get the club pros out of town. They decided to sponsor tournaments in the south and west, far from their country clubs, and they sent their pros on the road. Whenever one threatened to quit "the tour" and come home, the rich guys would raise the tournament prize money and the pros would stay just a little bit longer.

The Touring Pro

Thus the golf tour evolved as a way for rich guys to keep their troubled marriages intact and to keep themselves from being fleeced of their fortunes by professional golf hustlers. Of course, as soon as the pros were safely out of their hair, they went back to their golf courses with a vengeance, leaving their golf-widowed wives as bored as ever. Which leads to the story of how the professional tennis tour began. But that's another book, isn't it?

Professional golfers today have little in common with the original tour-playing hustlers. These days, each touring pro is carefully manufactured in a golf professional factory in North Carolina. Each is tall, thin, and blond and has a swing that is mechanically perfect. Each one gets free clothes, free equipment, free cars, and free houses from the rich guys who own the companies that make these things and who are still afraid of being cuckolded by tan, good-looking golf pros.

The purses on the professional golf tour have gotten so big that nowadays a professional golfer doesn't even have to win any tournaments to make a spectacular living. Most of the time, he can stroll the fairways of some fabulous resort golf course, shoot around par, come in thirtieth, and still make about 4 bazillion dollars a year (and that's not counting endorsement money from company presidents who want him to stay away from their wives in the off-season, too).

Totally Tubular Golf: A TV Guide

Golf is a sport made for television. From the heart-racing sight of a middle-aged man in ugly pants strolling down the fairway to the incisive commentary of an announcer with a phony British accent describing how coura-geous it is to hit a 9-iron from the rough, the action never stops.

Plus, it takes professional golfers an average of ten hours to complete an eighteen-hole round of golf. This leaves ample time for commercials for products like Viagra, athlete's foot powder, and Gas-X. The Western Open, the second-oldest professional golf tournament in the world (first held in 1899) and one of the most prestigious events in all of golf, is now sponsored by Cialis, a pill for erectile dysfunction. (I must again point out that *I am not making this up*.) Apparently, America's marketing geniuses have determined that golf fans are itchy, gassy, and impotent.

The British Announcer

Each TV network that broadcasts U.S. golf tournaments employs an announcer from Great Britain. Oftentimes, this man's only qualification for the position is that he speaks in the kind of haughty, arrogant accent that makes Americans feel like they just farted in front of the Queen. Networks hire these guys to lend an air of authenticity to a tournament, as though the "Greater-Tri-Cities-Tang-Simulated-Orange-Breakfast-Drink Open" were an historic event and not just an excuse to sell middle age golf nuts boner pills.

These Limeys make cute, British-y comments like, "Oooh, a bit of bad luck there for the plucky lad with the loosely bound upsy-down niblick-mashie from the dreadful heather." This might sound good to a TV exec, but real Americans change the channel when they hear something that sounds like a cricket match.

The Mediocre Ex-Pro Announcers

The mediocre ex-pro announcers are all in the twilight years of careers so bad that they are actually happier to miss a cut than make one because their chances of making money on TV are so much better than if they were to try to finish the tournament. These guys don't know if they are has-beens or never-weres.

Like airline pilots, they all speak in a lazy Southern drawl as though they grew up in a Texas caddyshack instead of an exclusive northeastern country club and haven't had to so much as carry their own bag since they were twelve.

TV announcing is an excellent gig for the mediocre ex-pro. He sits in a tent watching TV monitors, swilling beer, and joking about how bad he played in this week's tournament and gets paid for it. Pro golfers are generally such boring human beings that if one of these guys possesses even the faintest glimmer of a personality, he can make big bucks by being a tell-it-like-it-is sports journalist, while still playing well enough to get $10,000 a pop for those Monday afternoon corporate outings.

The Roving Announcer

Recently, the TV networks have taken to sending one mediocre ex-pro announcer out of the beer tent and onto the golf course to get "up-close" coverage of the players. The announcers decide who gets stuck with this onerous task by swilling beer until someone has to go to the Porta Potty. Whoever gives up first, loses. This has led to some very embarrassing accidents in the beer tents.

The roving announcer's mission is to get really, really close to the pro and ask him important questions about strategy and grip pressure while the pro decides how in the hell he's going to play a ball that has come to rest on a half-eaten cheeseburger. This is exciting for viewers because they never can tell when the player will look straight into the camera and suggest loudly that the roving announcer has, shall we say, a disturbing and quite intimate relationship with his mother.

"He's in absolute jail here, folks," the roving announcer will say, when he sees the ball glued to the Velveeta. "He's got no chance—no chance!—to get to the green. Why, he'll probably roll over on his back and whine like a dog when he sees this lie. You know, if God, Arnold Palmer, and a battalion of Marine Corps engineers came in here with a Caterpillar tractor they couldn't get this ball out of here."

Then, when the pro lofts a shot between two trees, around a dogleg, and onto the green, the roving announcer will fall to his knees weeping and declare that the pope and several congressmen name the site a Holy Golf Shrine to which pilgrims could trek barefoot so they could see where Joe Corporate Visor made par to lock up the Cheez-Whiz Invitational. It's an emotionally draining job.

The Majors: Masters of the Universe

The pro golf tour consists of fifty tournaments and a two-week "Silly Season" made up of goofy made-for-TV events. These Silly Season tourneys are very different from regular season tournaments, in that they were created simply to sell as many products as possible on TV and to provide easy money for the players. (Cough, cough.)

Four times a year, however, things on the pro golf tour get a little more serious. I'm talking about the Majors. The major tournaments: the Masters, the U.S. Open, the British Open, and the PGA, are considered *the* most important events in the golf pantheon. Win one, and you will forever after be known as a true champion. No one can doubt your skills, no one can doubt your heart, once you've survived the crucible of pressure that is a major golf tournament. Win one and the world will know that you are no fluke! Except of course for Ben Curtis, Paul Lawrie, Steve Jones, Orville Moody, Sam Parks Jr., Herman Kaiser, Gay Brewer, Charles Coody, Wayne Grady, John Mahaffey, Walter Burkemo, and Vic Ghezzi.

The Masters

The great Bobby Jones began the Masters Tournament and remains its patron saint. Jones remained an amateur throughout his career because of his dedication to the spirit of sportsmanship, his belief in the purity of the game, and because he was extremely wealthy and believed that professional golfers were the lowest kind of scum.

A committee of the six remaining survivors of the Battle of Gettysburg run the Masters and have decreed that everything at the tournament be painted "Masters Green," from the refreshment stands to the Porta Potties. This can be very confusing for the people who work at the Masters, and it's why you should be *very* careful when buying a beer there.

The Augusta National Golf Course has wide fairways, no rough, few bunkers, and no OB. What makes the course so difficult is the knowledge that if you accidentally wear an outfit that doesn't include the color "Masters Green," the rules committee will send a half-dozen members of the Daughters of the Confederacy after you to bludgeon you about the head and neck with their parasols and force you to sing twenty choruses of "Dixie."

Each year the year's previous winner presents the winner of the Masters with the traditional green jacket. This is considered a great achievement and honor. Also, each year all the previous winners get together at a banquet in their green jackets and eat green food. Which is why nobody ever wins the Masters two years in a row.

The U.S. Open

Though the U.S. Open is played in June, qualifying begins each year in early January and is open to everyone on the planet, whether they play golf or not. Local, county, state, regional, and sectional qualifying rounds, which run for five months, reduce the field to the 42,000 players who begin teeing off before dawn on the first day. After two rounds, the field is cut to those 67 over par or better (and ties) and those not hopelessly lost in the eleven-foot deep rough.

SHLUNK!

The U.S. Open is administered by the United States Golf Association, an organization of very poor golfers who feel that the tournament should be less a test of golf skills and more a test of hunting for lost golf balls. These evil fellows chuckle gleefully at the thought of the best players in the world teeing off with 7-irons and lagging six-foot putts to keep from shooting over 100. The fairways at the U.S. Open are so narrow the players must walk down them single file; the rough is heavier than several parts of the Amazon rainforest; and the greens are so slick that players have been known to actually lose their footing and fall off of them.

The British Open

In its early years, either Olde Tom Morris or Young Tom Morris always won the British

Open. This was mostly because nobody ever entered the British Open but Olde Tom Morris and Young Tom Morris. Actually, the Morris boys never actually *told* anybody what the hell it was they were doing out there on the beach, which pretty much made the two of them a lock for first and second place.

In the years after golf came to the U.S., the British Open was almost always won by an American pro who would arrive two weeks early and immerse himself in the culture to prepare for the event. He would buy a tweed cap, drink warm beer, eat mutton, and learn to play the bump and run. He would hire a colorful ninety-seven-year-old local caddy who would squint through the smoke from his briar pipe and say, "Aye laddie, yee kin nae git ta thet grin wi' oot a wee bet more shillelagh" when he meant "Hit more club."

In recent years, American pros have quit playing the British Open in droves. They don't wish to waste two valuable weeks of their careers on history and tradition when they could be playing a lucrative exhibition round with executives from the food additive industry. And who can blame them? Warm beer and mutton. Ugh.

The PGA

The last major tournament of the year is the PGA, for which every single professional golfer in the country is eligible—even the toothless seventy-eight-year-old guy who owns the local miniature golf course and whose main experience with tournament golf is handing out free game cards to any kid who gets an ace on the clown hole.

What usually happens at the PGA is that one of these obscure local pros shoots a 68 in the first round to lead the field. After answering questions from curious sportswriters in the press tent (like "Just who in God's name are *you*?"), the obscure club pro will be descended upon by major international corporations eager to be represented by such an inspiring up-from-his-own-bootstraps kind of fellow. By Friday's round, the obscure club pro will have company names on his shirt, hat, bag, shoes, and caddy, and tattooed on all visible parts of his body.

Touring pros always love when this happens, and they'll offer the club pro lots of friendly help and advice (like "Boy, it's great the way you hit it so square with that funny hitch in your backswing!"). Unused to the pressure—and to the extra weight of the advertisements now sewn to his body—the obscure club pro inevitably shoots 106 and the PGA is eventually won by the usual anonymous touring pro.

MOSTLY, I'D LIKE TO THANK MY AGENT, WHO STRUCTURED MY ENDORSEMENT CONTRACTS TO INCLUDE BIG BONUSES FOR A MAJOR TOURNAMENT WIN!!

Golfspeak:
A Glossary of Terms, Definitions, and Swear Words

Alligator
1. Animal native to Florida that lives in water hazards and preys on golfers trying to retrieve balls. 2. Animal native to expensive golf shirts.

Athlete's Foot
The only part of a golfer that is actually athletic.

Attitude Adjuster

Beer, or other adult beverage, consumed for the purpose of improving one's outlook on the back nine.

Bag Tag

Plastic ornament attached to golf bag to indicate courses where bag owner has played. Number of bag tags is generally in direct inverse proportion to ability.

Ball Washer

Golf course device that promotes the efficient evaporation of water.

Barbeque

Something people who live next to golf courses never do.

Bogie

1. One over par. 2. *Casablanca*.

Break

1. Amount of "turn" in a putt, as in "I think it breaks six inches to the left." 2. What golfer does to putter after said putt breaks six inches to the *right*.

Breeze

Any wind under 50 mph, as in "Let's not quit just because of this little breeze!"

Casual Water

Any wet place on the course in which *your* ball lands. (See *Water Hazard.*)

Cup

1. Plastic liner in hole. 2. Container for Attitude Adjuster.

Double Bogie

1. Two over par. 2. *Casablanca*, *The Maltese Falcon*.

Duck

1. Migratory bird that inhabits water hazards and quacks in golfer's backswings. 2. What people who live next to golf courses and still attempt to barbeque do frequently.

Fade

1. A shot that curves slightly from left to right, favored by many pros. 2. What the average player does after playing the first four holes in 2 under par.

Fence

1. Barrier separating golfers from irate homeowners. 2. Man who buys sets of golf clubs from frustrated players at ten cents on the dollar and later resells them for face value to the original owner.

Grip

1. Method of holding onto a golf club in a way that makes it nearly impossible to swing. 2. What a golfer loses after 3-putting from six feet.

103

TEED OFF!

Hacker

Any player in the group in front of you who plays slower than you think he should. (See *Maniac.*)

Halfway House

1. Place where golfers stop for rest and refreshment after the ninth hole. 2. Place where golfers who have been driven insane by the game and who have committed major felonies go to rehabilitate after serving out their prison terms.

Handicap

Statistical figure arrived at through a series of calculations indicating how much money a player thinks he can win from his opponents.

Head Cover

1. Knit or leather stocking designed to protect clubs. 2. Position golfer assumes upon hearing a cry of "fore."

Keeper

Any divot over six inches in length, suitable for keeping and planting in the backyard.

Lightning

God's way of telling you you've been playing too much golf.

Links

1. Early golf courses, named for their unique seaside configuration. 2. Style of chain fence designed so that golf balls can pass right through.

Locker Room

Area of clubhouse where golfers can change their clothes and their scorecards.

Maniac

Any player in the group behind you playing faster than you would like. (See *Hacker.*)

Rough

1. Long grass on either side of the fairway where most tee shots land. 2. Surface of a club that has been dragged across the parking lot.

Sand Wedge

An iron designed to enable a golfer to move huge amounts of sand from directly beneath a golf ball without actually touching it.

FUMPF!

Shank

1. A ball hit directly sideways. 2. The part of the club buried in the ground after this shot.

Snickers

1. Candy bar eaten at the halfway house. 2. Sound made by caddies watching your swing.

Sprinkler

Watering device built into fairways designed to automatically spray the area whenever a player is within ten feet.

Stroke

1. Attempt to advance the ball with a swing. 2. Seizure brought on by attempts to advance the ball with a swing.

Tee Marker

Objects designating the teeing area set up at an angle that makes it impossible to hit a straight tee shot.

Tee Plant

The act of driving a tee into the ground in the hopes that someday a tee tree will grow there.

Triple Bogie

1. Three over par. 2. *Casablanca*, *The Maltese Falcon*, *The African Queen*.

Water Hazard

Any wet place on the course where your opponent's ball lands. (See *Casual Water.*)

Wind

Weather phenomenon created by a player who has too many beers and chili dogs at the halfway house.

Yardage

1. Measurement used by courses to estimate distance of holes, usually accurate. 2. Measurement used by players to estimate distance of shots, usually inaccurate.

Yips

1. Affliction that causes you to tremble, twitch, and sweat profusely over short, important putts. 2. Sound your opponent makes when you miss a short, important putt.

The Ten Commandments of Modern Golf

ONE

Thou shalt not carry a ball retriever.

If you hit your ball into a water hazard, *it is gone*! Do not hold up the whole course so you can search around in the muck for a couple of yellowed, waterlogged X-outs. If you can't afford to lose a ball or two, you can't afford to play the game.

TWO

Thou shalt carry thy clubs in a suitable bag.

Your bag should house no less than two dozen balls, three sweaters, a rain suit, an umbrella, eight old gloves, a swing weight, six hundred tees, a ball marker, spare spikes, ten old scorecards, five broken pencils, a can of insect repellent, Band-Aids, a roll of toilet paper, and a tuna sandwich.

THREE

Thou shalt not let groups "hit up" on par-threes.

"Hitting up" was begun by the early Scots to see how many people they could hit with their flying featheries. This *did* thin out the number of players clogging up the courses, but otherwise it's dangerous and a waste of time.

FOUR

Thou shalt not use the word "golf" as a verb.

You do not "golf." You "play golf." The rules committee will soundly paddle players who use the word golf in this manner.

FIVE

Thou shalt not walk.

Are you crazy? You could have a heart attack! Besides, you need a cart to put your beer cooler in.

SIX

Thou shalt not play golf with thy spouse.

Unless thou would liketh a quick and nasty divorce.

SEVEN

Thou shalt not describe thy round in excruciating detail.

If you force someone in the bar to go all eighteen holes with you, you are required to pay him caddie fees.

EIGHT

Thou shalt not step in thy opponent's line.

Unless you're absolutely sure you can get away with it.

NINE

Thou shalt honor thy golf pro.

Hey, he's figured out how to make a living playing a game while you still can't break 100. Break down and buy a shirt from the pro shop once in a while, you cheapskate. First, though, make sure he's not sleeping with your wife.

TEN

Thou shalt keep holy the Sabbath.

Never miss your Sunday tee time. I don't know who built the church, but God made the grass and the sunshine and that tree you lie four behind. So enjoy.

About the Author

Tom Carey is a writer and illustrator living in northeast Ohio, whose previously published work includes *The Marriage Dictionary* and *How to Throw a Golf Club.* He plays lots of golf and only breaks a club if it really, really deserves it.